Trees

WONDER STARTERS

Trees

Illustrated by Esme Eve

Published by WONDER BOOKS
A Division of Grosset & Dunlap, Inc.
A Filmways Company
51 Madison Avenue   New York, N.Y. 10010

About Wonder Starters

Wonder Starters are vocabulary controlled information books for young children. More than ninety per cent of the words in the text will be in the reading vocabulary of the vast majority of young readers. Word and sentence length have also been carefully controlled.

Key new words associated with the topic of each book are repeated with picture explanations in the Starters dictionary at the end. The dictionary can also be used as an index for teaching children to look things up.

Teachers and experts have been consulted on the content and accuracy of the books.

Published in the United States by Wonder Books, a Division of Grosset & Dunlap, Inc.

Library of Congress Catalog Card Number: 76-50361
ISBN: 0-448-09697-8 (Trade Edition)
ISBN: 0-448-06455-3 (Library Edition)

First U.S. Printing 1977

© Macdonald and Company (Publishers),
Limited, 1971, London.

Printed and bound in the United States of America.

This is our tree.
We are building a house
in the branches.

1

We put leaves on the roof.
A squirrel watches us.
He lives in the tree.

2

The squirrel eats acorns.
Acorns grow on the tree.
Oak trees have acorns.
Our tree is an oak tree.

The squirrel hides acorns in the oak tree.
He keeps some in his home.
His home is called a drey.
His drey is made of twigs and leaves.

4

Some acorns fall on damp ground.
The seeds in these acorns start to grow.
Shoots grow up.
Roots grow down into the ground.

5

The seed grows into a little oak tree.
At first the stem grows leaves.
Then branches begin to grow.
6

Trees need water to grow.
They take in water with their roots.
They need sunshine too.
The sun shines on their leaves.

In the autumn the leaves die.
They change color.
The wind blows them down.
Then winter comes.

After winter comes the spring.
In spring it is warmer.
The buds on the twigs swell.
They grow into leaves.

9

This is an oak forest.
The oak trees let light through.
Flowers need light to grow.
Flowers grow on the ground.
10

This is a forest of pine trees.
It is very dark. Few flowers can grow.
There is a lovely smell.
The ground is covered with pine needles.

Pine needles are long thin leaves.
Pine tree seeds are in the pine cones.
The seeds and cones fall to the ground.

12

Pines and spruces stay green in winter.
They are evergreens.
Some evergreens make
good Christmas trees.

The men are cutting down a big tree.
They cut it with a saw.
The tree falls down.

14

Now you can see ring marks
where the trunk has been cut.
The number of rings
show the age of the tree.

Trucks and tractors bring the big logs
to the sawmill.
Big saws cut the logs into planks.
16

People make all kinds of things
out of wood.
All of these things are made from wood.

17

Some trees are very big.
This redwood tree is enormous.
You can drive through the trunk.

Palm trees grow in hot places.
There are many kinds of palm trees.
Two kinds are date and coconut palms.

19

Cocoa beans grow on trees.
Bananas grow on trees.
Oranges grow on trees too.

20

Rubber comes from rubber trees.
Lots of things are made of rubber.

See for yourself

Look at this picture.
There are forty things
made from wood.
See if you can find them all.

Starter's **Trees** words

branch
(page 1)

leaf
(page 2)

squirrel
(page 2)

acorn
(page 3)

oak tree
(page 3)

drey
(page 4)

twig
(page 4)

root
(page 5)

bud
(page 9)

forest
(page 10)

pine tree
(page 11)

pine cone
(page 12)

saw
(page 14)

trunk
(page 15)

tractor
(page 16)

logs
(page 16)

sawmill
(page 16)

plank
(page 16)

palm tree
(page 19)

dates
(page 19)

cocoa beans
(page 20)

bananas
(page 20)

oranges
(page 20)

rubber tree
(page 21)

24